PAUL ROMANUK

HOCKEY SUPERSTARS

2014-2015

Your complete guide to the 2014–2015 season,
featuring action photos of
your favorite players

SCHOLASTIC
TORONTO NEW YORK LONDON AUCKLAND SYDNEY
MEXICO CITY NEW DELHI HONG KONG BUENOS AIRES

THE TEAMS

WESTERN CONFERENCE – PACIFIC DIVISION

CALGARY FLAMES
team colors: red, gold, black and white
home arena: Scotiabank Saddledome
mascot: Harvey the Hound
Stanley Cups won: 1

EDMONTON OILERS
team colors: white, royal blue and orange
home arena: Rexall Place
Stanley Cups won: 5

ANAHEIM DUCKS
team colors: black, gold, orange and white
home arena: Honda Center
mascot: Wild Wing
Stanley Cups won: 1

LOS ANGELES KINGS
team colors: white, black and silver
home arena: Staples Center
mascot: Bailey
Stanley Cups won: 2

PHOENIX COYOTES
team colors: red, black, sand and white
home arena: Jobing.com Arena
mascot: Howler

VANCOUVER CANUCKS
team colors: blue, silver, green and white
home arena: Rogers Arena
mascot: Fin

SAN JOSE SHARKS
team colors: teal, black, orange and white
home arena: SAP Center at San Jose
mascot: S.J. Sharkie

WESTERN CONFERENCE – CENTRAL DIVISION

CHICAGO BLACKHAWKS
nickname: Hawks
team colors: red, black and white
home arena: United Center
mascot: Tommy Hawk
Stanley Cups won: 5

COLORADO AVALANCHE
nickname: Avs
team colors: burgundy, silver, black, blue and white
home arena: Pepsi Center
mascot: Bernie
Stanley Cups won: 2

DALLAS STARS
team colors: green, white, black and silver
home arena: American Airlines Center
Stanley Cups won: 1

NASHVILLE PREDATORS
nickname: Preds
team colors: dark blue, white and gold
home arena: Bridgestone Arena
mascot: Gnash

MINNESOTA WILD
team colors: red, green, gold, wheat and white
home arena: Xcel Energy Center
mascot: Nordy

WINNIPEG JETS
team colors: dark blue, blue, gray, silver, red and white
home arena: MTS Centre
mascot: Mick E. Moose

ST. LOUIS BLUES
team colors: blue, gold, dark blue and white
home arena: Scottrade Center
mascot: Louie

EASTERN CONFERENCE – ATLANTIC DIVISION

TORONTO MAPLE LEAFS
nickname: Leafs
team colors: blue and white
home arena: Air Canada Centre
mascot: Carlton the Bear
Stanley Cups won: 11
· · · · · · · · · · · · · · · · · ·

BUFFALO SABRES
team colors: navy blue, gold, silver and white
home arena: First Niagara Center
mascot: Sabretooth
· · · · · · · · · · · · · · · · · ·

FLORIDA PANTHERS
nickname: Cats
team colors: red, navy blue, yellow, gold and white
home arena: BB&T Center
mascot: Stanley C. Panther

OTTAWA SENATORS
nickname: Sens
team colors: black, red, gold and white
home arena: Canadian Tire Centre
mascot: Spartacat
Stanley Cups won:
7 (pre-1934 team)
· · · · · · · · · · · · · · · · · ·

TAMPA BAY LIGHTNING
nickname: Bolts
team colors: blue, black and white
home arena: Tampa Bay Times Forum
mascot: ThunderBug
Stanley Cups won: 1

MONTREAL CANADIENS
nickname: Habs
team colors: red, blue and white
home arena: Bell Centre
mascot: Youppi
Stanley Cups won: 24
· · · · · · · · · · · · · · · · · ·

DETROIT RED WINGS
nickname: Wings
team colors: red and white
home arena: Joe Louis Arena
mascot (unofficial): Al the Octopus
Stanley Cups won: 11
· · · · · · · · · · · · · · · · · ·

BOSTON BRUINS
nickname: Bs
team colors: gold, black and white
home arena: TD Garden
mascot: Blades the Bruin
Stanley Cups won: 6

EASTERN CONFERENCE – METROPOLITAN DIVISION

NEW YORK RANGERS
nickname: Blueshirts
team colors: blue, white and red
home arena: Madison Square Garden
Stanley Cups won: 4
· · · · · · · · · · · · · · · · · ·

COLUMBUS BLUE JACKETS
nickname: Jackets
team colors: blue, red, silver and white
home arena: Nationwide Arena
mascot: Stinger
· · · · · · · · · · · · · · · · · ·

CAROLINA HURRICANES
nickname: Canes
team colors: red, black, gray and white
home arena: PNC Arena
mascot: Stormy
Stanley Cups won: 1

NEW YORK ISLANDERS
nickname: Isles
team colors: orange, blue and white
home arena: Nassau Veterans Memorial Coliseum
mascot: Sparky the Dragon
Stanley Cups won: 4
· · · · · · · · · · · · · · · · · ·

PITTSBURGH PENGUINS
nickname: Pens
team colors: black, gold and white
home arena: Consol Energy Center
mascot: Iceburgh
Stanley Cups won: 3

PHILADELPHIA FLYERS
team colors: orange, white and black
home arena: Wells Fargo Center
Stanley Cups won: 2
· · · · · · · · · · · · · · · · · ·

NEW JERSEY DEVILS
team colors: red, black and white
home arena: Prudential Center
mascot: N.J. Devil
Stanley Cups won: 3
· · · · · · · · · · · · · · · · · ·

WASHINGTON CAPITALS
nickname: Caps
team colors: red, navy blue and white
home arena: Verizon Center
mascot: Slapshot

YOUR FAVORITE TEAM

Name of your favorite team: _____

Conference and division: _____

Players on your favorite team at the start of the season:

Number	Name	Position
_____	_____	_____
_____	_____	_____
_____	_____	_____
_____	_____	_____
_____	_____	_____
_____	_____	_____
_____	_____	_____
_____	_____	_____
_____	_____	_____
_____	_____	_____
_____	_____	_____
_____	_____	_____
_____	_____	_____

Changes, Trades, New Players

_____   _____   _____
_____   _____   _____
_____   _____   _____
_____   _____   _____
_____   _____   _____
_____   _____   _____
_____   _____   _____

End-of-Season Standings

Fill in the name of the team you think will finish in first place in each of the four NHL Divisions.

WESTERN CONFERENCE

_____ **PACIFIC DIVISION**

_____ **CENTRAL DIVISION**

EASTERN CONFERENCE

ATLANTIC DIVISION _____

METROPOLITAN DIVISION _____

The Playoffs

Which two teams will meet in the Stanley Cup Final? Fill in their names below, then circle the team you think will win.

Eastern Conference Winner: _____

Western Conference Winner: _____

YOUR FAVORITE TEAM

Your Team — All Season Long

The standings of hockey teams are listed at NHL.com and on the sports pages of the newspaper all season long. The standings will show you which team is in first place, second place, etc., right down to last place.

Some of the abbreviations you'll become familiar with are: GP for games played; W for wins; L for losses; OT for overtime losses; PTS for points; A for assists; G for goals.

Check the standings on the same day of every month and copy down what they say about your team. By keeping track of your team this way you'll be able to see when it was playing well and when it wasn't.

	GP	W	L	OT	PTS
NOVEMBER 1					
DECEMBER 1					
JANUARY 1					
FEBRUARY 1					
MARCH 1					
APRIL 1					
MAY 1					

Final Standings

At the end of the season print the final record of your team below.

YOUR TEAM	GP	W	L	OT	PTS

Your Favorite Players' Scoring Records

While you're keeping track of your favorite team during the season, you can also follow the progress of your favorite players. Just fill in their point totals on the same day of every month.

player	nov 1	dec 1	jan 1	feb 1	mar 1	apr 1	may 1

Your Favorite Goaltenders' Records

You can keep track of your favorite goaltenders' averages during the season. Just fill in the information below.

GAA is the abbreviation for goals-against average. That's the average number of goals given up by a goaltender during a game over the course of the season.

goaltender	nov 1	dec 1	jan 1	feb 1	mar 1	apr 1	may 1

WINNIPEG JETS

Dustin Byfuglien is tough not to notice. He's physically bigger than most NHL players, his shot is better than many other players' and, on top of all of that, he can excel as either a defenseman or a forward. It's that last point that got him a lot of attention last season when coach Paul Maurice moved him up from the blueline to play forward. The move was the subject of a lot of debate among fans and media, but for Dustin it was just a matter of doing whatever he was being asked to do.

"I prefer playing D a little more," said Dustin, "but it doesn't really matter as long as I'm playing. That's the most important thing."

"He [Dustin] can play both positions and excel at both positions. He's that good," said coach Maurice at the time. "We're putting an elite player in either of those two roles, up front or at the back end."

Certainly playing up front brings back fond memories for the player they call Big Buff. He played forward for the Chicago Blackhawks during their Stanley Cup Championship in 2010. Dustin was moved from defense to forward during the playoffs, and he went on to play

a big role with the club. In the Western Conference Final he scored the game-winning goal in three of Chicago's four wins.

"There's something about the playoffs that makes you have that extra spark," said Dustin. "In the playoffs you have to be ready to go every night."

"A lot of memories run through your head. What got you there. It's funny, but the Cup doesn't feel that heavy."
— Dustin talks about what it was like to lift the Stanley Cup in 2010

Whether it is the playoffs or the regular season, Dustin has a knack for scoring important goals — he was one of the Jets' top power play performers last season with eight power play goals.

"You gotta be in the right spot at the right time. Take your time, shoot the puck. Get it on net. That's all you have to do sometimes, just get it on net."

That's great advice for young players to follow whether they're forwards or defensemen. Or, as in Dustin's case, either.

DID YOU KNOW?

Dustin is an avid fisherman. In the off-season you'll often find him casting a rod someplace, trying to haul in a big one. He's even competed in pro fishing tournaments.

HOCKEY MEMORIES

One of the biggest influences on Dustin's career was his grandfather, who Dustin recalls was always excited to see new places and to drive him to his games wherever they may have been. "It was fun that he was always there."

2013–2014 STATS

GP	G	A	PTS	PIM
78	20	36	56	86

Chicago Blackhawks' 8th choice, 245th overall, in 2003 NHL Entry Draft
1st NHL Team, Season: Chicago Blackhawks, 2005–2006
Born: March 27, 1985, in Minneapolis, Minnesota
Position: Defense/Right Wing
Shoots: Right
Height: 1.95 m (6'5")
Weight: 120 kg (265 lbs.)

SIDNEY CROSBY

PITTSBURGH PENGUINS

He's a champion, a leader and, in the minds of most, the biggest hockey superstar on the planet. Sidney Crosby, heading into his 10th NHL season, was dominant last year with the Penguins. He won his second NHL scoring title, his third Lester B. Pearson/Ted Lindsay Award (for the league's most valuable player as voted by fellow players) and his second Hart Trophy as the NHL MVP. Late in the season, when asked about Sidney's chances of winning the Hart, then-coach Dan Bylsma had to think for about one second before he answered.

"I don't think there's any question. This season I don't think it's even close. I think there's no question. I think he's skating away with it."

"I don't think there's ever a time when I step back and say I wish I was something different. I'm doing what I love to do."

Sidney topped the 100-point mark for the fifth time in his nine-season career, and he is on track to hit 800 career points this season. Perhaps just as significantly, last season saw Sid play in 80 regular-season games. It was only the second time in his career that he managed to accomplish that, and it came after a couple of seasons where he struggled with several injuries, including concussions. There were times when many wondered whether he would ever recover from the concussion symptoms, including Sidney himself.

"I'd be lying if I didn't say that I thought about it," Sidney said in an interview with the CBC. "With concussions, you feel like you're getting better, and it can be one day and you're back to where you started."

You don't have to be a Pittsburgh Penguins fan to be happy to see Sidney out on the ice, looking better than ever. Hockey fans everywhere, of any team, should appreciate all that he brings to the game. Let's all hope he can continue to do that for many more years.

DID YOU KNOW?
Sidney's sister, Taylor, is a goalie and has attended a couple of elite development camps with Hockey Canada. She hopes to follow in her older brother's path and play in the Olympics one day.

HOCKEY MEMORIES
During his rookie season, Sidney started off playing alongside Hall of Famer and future Penguins owner Mario Lemieux. Sid has great memories of those early NHL days with Lemieux and says it "made a big difference, especially early on in my career."

2013–2014 STATS

GP	G	A	PTS	PIM
80	36	68	104	46

Pittsburgh Penguins' 1st choice, 1st overall, in 2005 NHL Entry Draft
1st NHL Team, Season: Pittsburgh Penguins, 2005–2006
Born: August 7, 1987, in Cole Harbour, Nova Scotia
Position: Center
Shoots: Left
Height: 1.80 m (5'11")
Weight: 90.5 kg (200 lbs.)

TAMPA BAY LIGHTNING

Sometimes a superstar player brings more to a team than what is simply seen on the ice by the fans. Goals, assists, plus-minus numbers all say something about a player's contribution, of course. But numbers don't tell you about a player's personality and how it can affect the team. Those things can be just as important as points.

Valtteri Filppula left the Detroit Red Wings in July 2013 as a free agent and signed a five-year deal with the Tampa Bay Lightning. A new deal for Valtteri wasn't something the Red Wings could fit into their financial planning, so he parted ways with the only NHL team he had ever played for. While teammates and coaches missed his on-ice contributions, they also missed his personality.

> "It was tough to leave Detroit, but coming to Tampa Bay has been good. It's been a lot of fun. I feel like we have a good team and a great bunch of guys."

"Valtteri was a great player for many, many years for us," said former Detroit teammate Niklas Kronwall. "But, just as important,

he was a good person and a great guy in the room."

During his NHL career, Valtteri has generally been looked upon as a solid two-way player, meaning that he can be a scorer and playmaker, but is counted on just as heavily for his sound defensive play. That perception changed a little last season. Tampa Bay's top center, Steve Stamkos, went down with a broken tibia early in the season and Valtteri was suddenly expected to contribute some of the offense his injured teammate couldn't. He responded with one of his best offensive seasons ever — 25 goals, 33 assists for 58 points.

"When Stamkos was hurt, he was the guy we counted on to carry the load up the middle," said former teammate Martin St. Louis. "The guy's been a big addition to the team. He's got a pretty high hockey IQ, he's fun to watch and he's a great guy off the ice."

Valtteri's contributions were part of a Stanley Cup Championship in Detroit in 2008, and he's hoping to contribute to one in Tampa. On the ice, off the ice — whatever it takes.

DID YOU KNOW?
Valtteri is one of the top faceoff men in the NHL. Last season he led Tampa Bay in that stat, winning 52.3% of his faceoffs.

HOCKEY MEMORIES
Winning the Stanley Cup with the Detroit Red Wings in 2008 is Valtteri's greatest professional hockey memory so far. The memory was made even sweeter because he contributed 5 goals and 6 assists during Detroit's great playoff run.

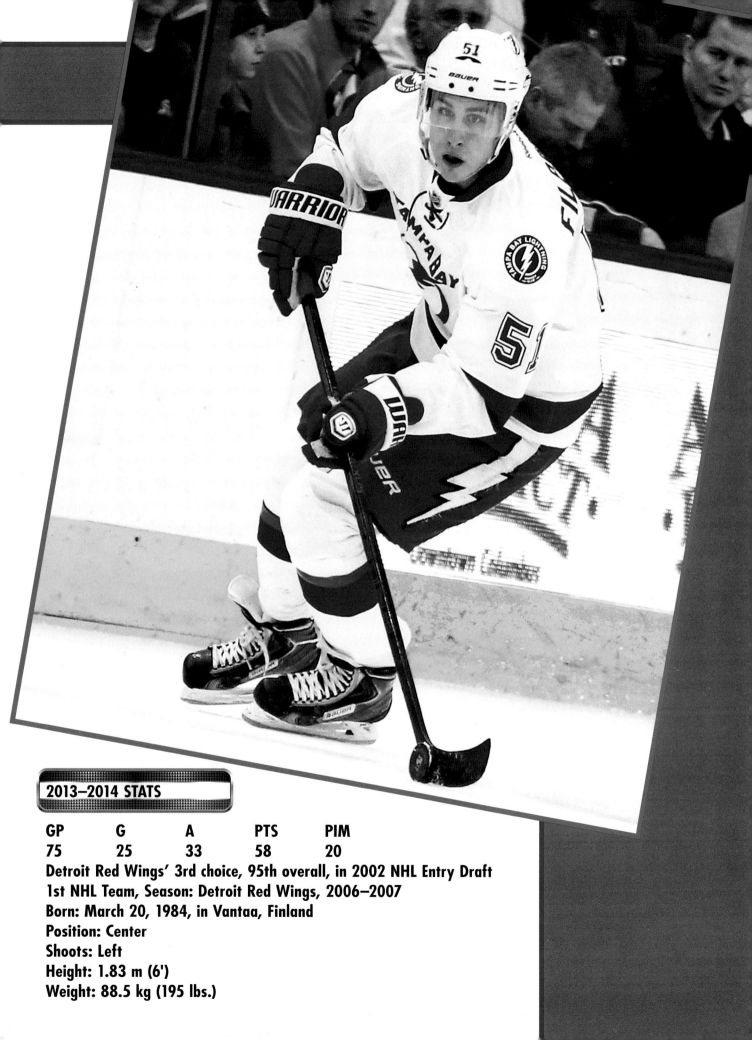

2013–2014 STATS

GP	G	A	PTS	PIM
75	25	33	58	20

Detroit Red Wings' 3rd choice, 95th overall, in 2002 NHL Entry Draft
1st NHL Team, Season: Detroit Red Wings, 2006–2007
Born: March 20, 1984, in Vantaa, Finland
Position: Center
Shoots: Left
Height: 1.83 m (6')
Weight: 88.5 kg (195 lbs.)

RYAN GETZLAF

ANAHEIM DUCKS

It's difficult to decide which is more impressive: Ryan Getzlaf scoring 600 career points, or the fact that he scored them all with one team — the only team he's ever played for in the NHL — the Anaheim Ducks. Most players who play for as long as Ryan has (he's heading into his 10th NHL season) end up playing for at least a couple of different clubs. As for the 600 career points, only 294 other players in the history of the NHL have hit that mark. Ryan hit the career milestone last season, with a goal and two assists in a game on March 23, 2014, against the Florida Panthers. It was the 623rd game of his career.

"I've always envisioned myself playing for one team, especially this organization, it's been great to me."

"I didn't know about it [the milestone] until after, but it's one of those things. It's another step along the way here, playing in one organization," said Ryan after the game.

Ryan, who finished second in balloting for the Hart Trophy as NHL MVP last season, is typical of many great players in that he's never lost the love of playing the game to simply have fun.

"I was in love with the game since I was four," Ryan said. "I was in love with playing the game, and I think that every spare moment that I had to play, I played."

That passion has fueled his success. He's played, and he's won — a World Junior Hockey Championship, two Olympic gold medals and a Stanley Cup Championship. And he continues to improve. Last season Ryan hit the 30-goal mark for the first time in his career, as he put together his highest point total since 2008–2009's career high 91-point effort.

"I've always said that there's no reason why he couldn't be the best player in the league," said Teemu Selanne. "He can be as good as he wants to be. It's scary."

It goes to show you how far you can go with talent, a passion for the game and a team that wants you there for the long, and in this case successful, run.

DID YOU KNOW?

Ryan isn't just a hockey guy. When he has the time, he loves to golf, wakeboard or play a bit of beach volleyball — and he once took batting practice with the Los Angeles Angels.

HOCKEY MEMORIES

Like many Canadian hockey players, Ryan has fond memories of playing in the World Junior Championship for his country. He was part of Canada's silver medal team in 2004 and won gold in 2005.

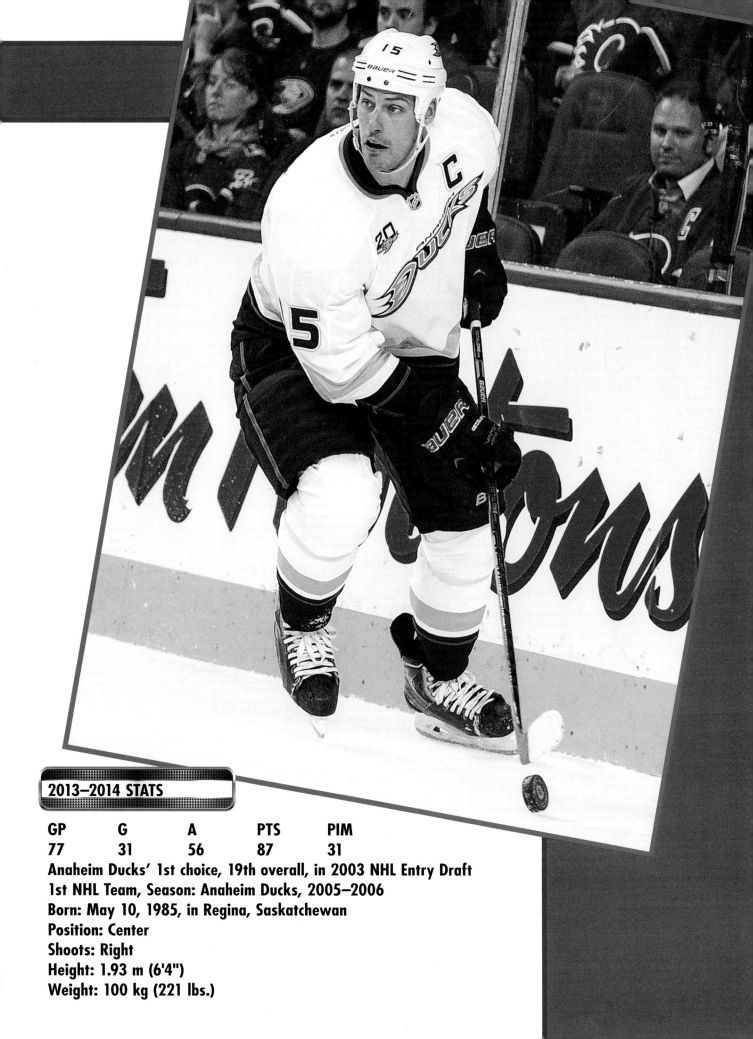

2013–2014 STATS

GP	G	A	PTS	PIM
77	31	56	87	31

Anaheim Ducks' 1st choice, 19th overall, in 2003 NHL Entry Draft
1st NHL Team, Season: Anaheim Ducks, 2005–2006
Born: May 10, 1985, in Regina, Saskatchewan
Position: Center
Shoots: Right
Height: 1.93 m (6'4")
Weight: 100 kg (221 lbs.)

TOMAS HERTL

Tomas Hertl is excited about this season, his second in the NHL. It's not that last season didn't have its high points, it's just that it was cut a little short.

Tomas had been playing in the Czech Republic's top league as a teenager for two seasons, holding his own against players with much more experience, when he was drafted in the first round by the San Jose Sharks. Tomas made the team coming out of training camp and looked sharp in his first couple of outings. He picked up an assist in his first NHL game and followed up with a pair of goals in his second.

But it was his third game that put him on the radar. The Sharks were on a roll as they caught the New York Rangers on an off night and hammered them 9–2, and Tomas scored four of those goals. The last goal was the one that had fellow players talking with one another about how amazing it was. As he swooped in on goal, Tomas slipped the puck back through his legs. Then, moving the stick back between his legs and keeping the puck on his forehand, he flicked the puck in behind Rangers goalie Martin Biron. It was one of the most spectacular goals scored last season; the crowd in San Jose went crazy as Hertl celebrated.

"It's the NHL, my dream. Unbelievable," Tomas told reporters afterward.

"I haven't seen a goal like that in a game, probably ever."
—TV analyst Barry Melrose on Hertl's "between the legs" goal.

By December Tomas was a leading candidate for the Calder Trophy as NHL Rookie of the Year. Then, on December 19, 2013, during a game against the L.A. Kings, Tomas suffered a knee injury in a collision with a Kings player and required surgery. In an instant, Tomas's season had turned from one of recognition to one of recovery.

Tomas was back on the ice in time to play for the Czech Republic in the World Hockey Championship in May. He looked good, with six points in nine games. All signs are pointing to an impressive, and hopefully injury free, second season with the Sharks.

DID YOU KNOW?

Tomas has an older brother, Jaroslav, and when Tomas played his first game in the Extraliga, the top league in the Czech Republic, they were put together on the same line. It was the first time the two had ever played together.

HOCKEY MEMORIES

Tomas says that when he was growing up in Prague he used to follow his favorite team, the Pittsburgh Penguins, and tried to pattern his game after his favorite player, Evgeni Malkin.

2013–2014 STATS

GP	G	A	PTS	PIM
37	15	10	25	4

San Jose Sharks' 1st choice, 17th overall, in 2012 NHL Entry Draft
1st NHL Team, Season: San Jose Sharks, 2013–2014
Born: November 12, 1993, in Prague, Czech Republic
Position: Center
Shoots: Left
Height: 1.88 m (6'2")
Weight: 95 kg (210 lbs.)

ERIK KARLSSON

Erik Karlsson's success is due to many of the usual things: talent, dedication and a lot of hard work. But another big reason for Erik's great success is the team that drafted him. The Ottawa Senators surprised some when they selected the small and relatively unknown defenseman from Sweden.

"Looking back, we saw a small body, but big-time skill," said Ottawa general manager Bryan Murray a few years later.

"If you want to be good, be successful, you have to be confident in yourself. When you play with confidence, that's when you play as good as you can."

On draft day, Erik was listed as being 180 cm (5'11"), 75 kg (165 lbs.). The average size of an NHL defenseman is just a little under 188 cm (6'2") with a weight of about 95 kg (210 lbs.). But while Erik lacked in size, he had exceptional speed and fantastic offensive skills. The question was, could one make up for the other? The early answer seemed to be no. Erik struggled in his first two seasons in the NHL, particularly in his second season when the team was poor and his plus-minus was a woeful minus 30. But the Senators stuck with Erik. He grew another inch, he gained weight and he became stronger and more able to cope physically with big NHL forwards. In his third season, Erik's hard work and the Senators' patience came together, and the result was a breakthrough season that saw him lead all NHL defensemen in scoring and take home the Norris Trophy as the league's top defenseman.

Last season saw Erik once again top all other NHL defensemen in points. He also starred for Sweden at the Olympics — finishing number one on his team in scoring and being named a tournament All-Star and Best Defenseman.

"It's been very important that they've let me take my time and play the game I do and never tried to make me into something I'm not," Erik said last season. "I'm very fortunate to be playing for a team that has allowed me to do that."

DID YOU KNOW?
During his rookie season in the NHL, Erik lived with teammate and Swedish hockey legend Daniel Alfredsson. The two became good friends and Erik credits Daniel with helping him to learn how to be a pro on and off the ice.

HOCKEY MEMORIES
Erik played for Sweden at the 2009 World Junior Hockey Championship in Ottawa. He remembers the "huge crowds, and seeing what it felt like to be a professional athlete playing in front of all those people."

2013–2014 STATS

GP	G	A	PTS	PIM
82	20	54	74	36

Ottawa Senators' 1st choice, 15th overall, in 2008 NHL Entry Draft
1st NHL Team, Season: Ottawa Senators, 2009–2010
Born: May 31, 1990, in Landsbro, Sweden
Position: Defense
Shoots: Right
Height: 1.83 m (6'0")
Weight: 81.5 kg (180 lbs.)

DUNCAN KEITH

CHICAGO BLACKHAWKS

The best athletes are rarely, if ever, satisfied. In 2009–2010 Duncan Keith won a gold medal with Canada at the Olympic Games and the Stanley Cup with the Chicago Blackhawks, and then was named the Norris Trophy winner as the best defenseman in the NHL. When asked how he could possibly top that, he was quick to answer: "Win some more. Win another Cup, win another medal. As a professional, you always want to keep improving; to do more."

"Being in the NHL is a privilege, and to stay here you have to have discipline and know how to carry yourself."

Although the Blackhawks didn't win the Cup last season, Duncan made good on two of his three goals: winning another gold medal with Canada at the Olympics and winning the Norris Trophy as the NHL's best defenseman. He finished up with 6 goals and 55 assists for 61 points, and he is showing no sign of losing a step as he heads into his 10th season with Chicago, making him the longest-serving player on the team.

Strange as it may seem, one of the NHL's best defensemen actually started his hockey life as a forward. Duncan played up front when he started minor hockey, but when he was 10 years old his coach decided to move him back to the blueline. Whether he was up front or playing defense, Duncan never stopped dreaming about making it to the NHL. After being drafted in the second round in the 2002 Entry Draft, Duncan had to persevere for another three years — one season in junior hockey and two in the minors — before he played his first NHL game, on October 5, 2005, against the Anaheim Ducks.

"Some people might have doubted me early in my career because of my size. They thought I was too small. That bothered me a bit, but that's what's great about sports. Everyone has opinions and it's best not to bother with them too much and just get out there and do your thing."

The approach has worked for Duncan. There's no doubt now that he's one of the best.

DID YOU KNOW?

Keith took a puck in the mouth during game four of the 2010 Western Conference Final against San Jose. He lost seven teeth, but was back out on the ice after a few shifts!

HOCKEY MEMORIES

Aside from the awards and championships and trophies, some of Duncan's most cherished memories are of his mom, who worked as a nurse's helper, dropping him at practice first thing in the morning. She'd watch for a little while before she had to rush off to work.

2013–2014 STATS

GP	G	A	PTS	PIM
79	6	55	61	28

Chicago Blackhawks' 2nd choice, 54th overall, in 2002 NHL Entry Draft
1st NHL Team, Season: Chicago Blackhawks, 2005–2006
Born: July 16, 1983, in Winnipeg, Manitoba
Position: Defense
Shoots: Left
Height: 1.85 m (6'1")
Weight: 90.5 kg (200 lbs.)

PHIL KESSEL

Despite the up and down fortunes of the Toronto Maple Leafs, their top scorer and best player has been pretty consistent at doing exactly what he's supposed to do — score. The Leafs traded for Phil Kessel just prior to the start of the 2009–2010 season. They sent two first-round draft picks and a second-round pick to the Boston Bruins for a player they hoped would be the team's offensive leader for years to come. In five seasons with the Leafs, Phil has more than upheld his part of the bargain — leading the team in scoring in every one of those seasons, including last season's total of 80 points.

Phil does most of his talking on the ice; when he does do interviews he prefers to talk about how the team is playing, rather than his own game.

"It's a team game and the only way any individual is going to have success is if his teammates have success as well," says Phil.

What Phil has is the ability to make others around him better. Toronto teammates Tyler Bozak and James van Riemsdyk both enjoyed career-best seasons last year skating alongside him.

"He's our best player, and so when he's going I think it filters through the lineup and makes everyone go a little harder," Bozak told a group of TV reporters after a game last season.

"He's my favorite player to watch, partly because he's my brother, but also I think he's just awesome. A lot of people think we look exactly alike out there."
—Amanda Kessel, talking about her brother and their similar playing styles

---

Phil comes from a great hockey family. His sister, Amanda, is a star with the U.S. Women's National Team and his brother, Blake, plays in the minors. Both Phil and Amanda represented the U.S. at the 2014 Winter Olympics and both are being counted on to be key players with their respective national teams for many years.

Whether he has the Toronto Maple Leaf on his sweater, or the U.S. red, white and blue, Phil will continue to do what he does best: score goals.

DID YOU KNOW?
Phil spent two years with the prestigious U.S. National Team Development Program in Ann Arbor, Michigan. He left the program as the all-time leading scorer in the history of the program, with 180 points and 102 goals in two seasons.

HOCKEY MEMORIES
Many Kessel Christmases featured an afternoon game of outdoor hockey with relatives and friends during which, the story goes, the three Kessel kids weren't allowed to be on the same team.

2013–2014 STATS

GP	G	A	PTS	PIM
82	37	43	80	27

Boston Bruins' 1st choice, 5th overall, in 2006 NHL Entry Draft
1st NHL Team, Season: Boston Bruins, 2006–2007
Born: October 2, 1987, in Madison, Wisconsin
Position: Right Wing
Shoots: Right
Height: 1.83 m (6'0")
Weight: 91.5 kg (202 lbs.)

NATHAN MACKINNON

COLORADO AVALANCHE

The word "expectation" and the name "Nathan MacKinnon" often appear in the same sentence. It has been this way for quite a few years now. As an atom hockey player Nathan scored 200 points during a 50-game season! He was a star as a AAA bantam player, despite playing against boys two or three years older than he was. Nathan was a first overall pick in the Quebec Major Junior Hockey League draft and led the Halifax Mooseheads to a Memorial Cup title. To cap it off, he was named the tournament's Most Valuable Player before being selected first overall in the NHL Entry Draft a few weeks later. There are those who saw it all coming.

"He was different. His skating was something that jumped out at me right away," Joel Greenwood, Nathan's coach when he was 11 years old, said before the 2013 draft. "He was keen and eager to learn . . . he wanted to become a complete player."

That great attitude and eagerness to learn continued last season, Nathan's rookie year in the NHL. His natural talent and work ethic caught the attention of Colorado fans and, more importantly, coach Patrick Roy. It wasn't uncommon to see the coach show confidence in the rookie by putting him on the ice in crucial situations. That's something that doesn't happen with many NHL rookies.

"I felt like I wanted to give him a little more because he was playing well," said Roy. "But on the other hand, we want to use this year to help build his confidence and his foundation. We want him to learn to play without the puck. We want him to play with confidence. That's why I try him in different situations."

"I feel as though I'm growing in every game. I'm realizing what I have to do to have good games at this level."

Nathan adapted to most of those situations and continued to improve. He led all NHL rookies in scoring on his way to winning the Calder Trophy. He also put in an appearance with Canada at the World Hockey Championship and looked good in his first international competition as a pro. Onward and upward for Nathan this season!

DID YOU KNOW?
Nathan grew up in a house about five minutes from where Sidney Crosby grew up in Cole Harbour, Nova Scotia. Nathan also went to the same prep school as Crosby: Shattuck-St. Mary's in Faribault, Minnesota.

HOCKEY MEMORIES
Nathan recalls it being "pretty awesome" to hear his name called out first by Colorado general manager Joe Sakic at the 2013 NHL Draft. As he stood to have his photo taken, he noticed he was standing between two Hall of Fame members — Sakic and coach Patrick Roy.

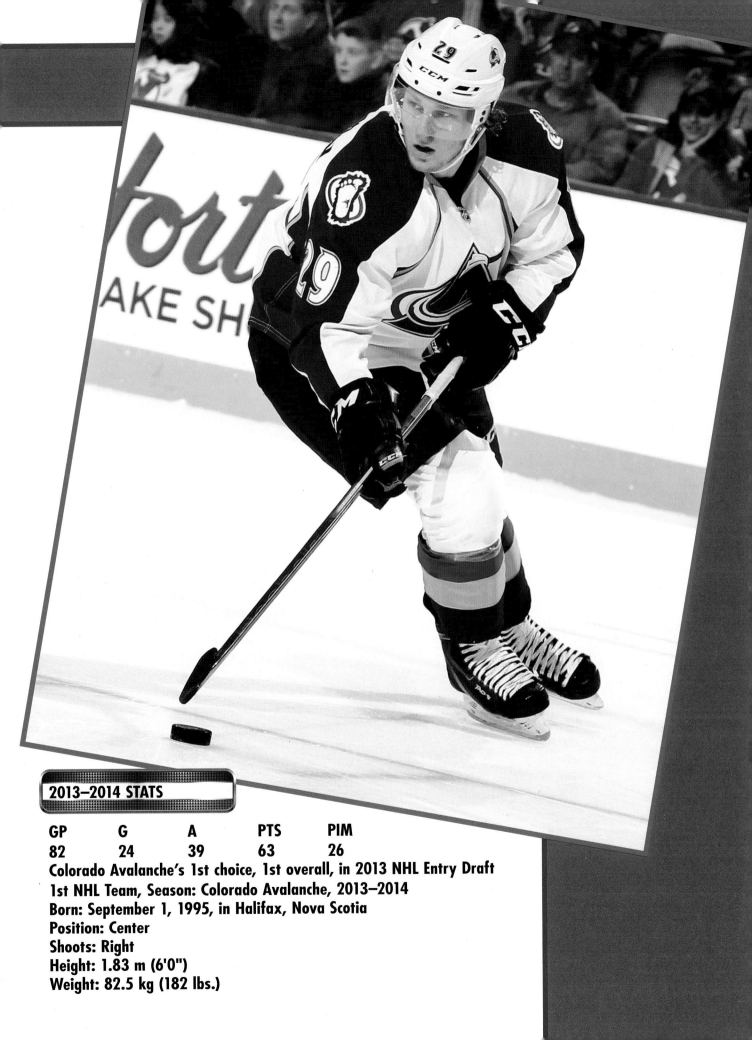

2013–2014 STATS

GP	G	A	PTS	PIM
82	24	39	63	26

Colorado Avalanche's 1st choice, 1st overall, in 2013 NHL Entry Draft
1st NHL Team, Season: Colorado Avalanche, 2013–2014
Born: September 1, 1995, in Halifax, Nova Scotia
Position: Center
Shoots: Right
Height: 1.83 m (6'0")
Weight: 82.5 kg (182 lbs.)

PATRICK MARLEAU

SAN JOSE SHARKS

In 1997, Patrick Marleau was the youngest player taken in the draft. He's gone on to play 16 seasons in a Sharks sweater, becoming the franchise's all-time leader in games played, goals scored and points scored. So it wasn't a big surprise when the Sharks decided to lock up Patrick for another three years by extending his contract in January of last season. It was, likewise, not a surprise that they also extended the contract of Patrick's good friend Joe Thornton at the same time.

> "You know, hockey is a humbling game. Just when you think you're getting things to go the right way, it throws another curve at you, so you've got to be ready at all times."

"Patrick and Joe continue to perform at an elite level in the National Hockey League and, most importantly, they make the other players around them better," said general manager Doug Wilson at the time of the signings.

Patrick is a rare breed in this era of professional sports, never mind professional hockey, with a career spanning more than 15 years, all of them with the same team.

Patrick was asked, when he played his 1000th career game with the Sharks a few seasons ago, whether or not he thought much about his longevity with one team.

"You don't really think about it too much until it just happens, and then everyone seems to make a big deal about it. But then, when you think about it you realize how hard it is to get there, and all of the support and all the things that go into it, from friends and family to the organization. Then it seems special."

When you look back at what he accomplished last season, Patrick looks as strong as ever: San Jose lost a tough seven-game first-round playoff battle with their rivals the L.A. Kings. Patrick was front and center as he led the team in scoring in the series with seven points. He finished third in team scoring during the regular season.

On top of his duties with the Sharks, Patrick played in his second Olympic Games for Canada and was a big part of the team's gold medal finish. Patrick heads into his 17th season with the Sharks still at the top of his game.

DID YOU KNOW?
Patrick opened the 2012–2013 season with four multi-goal games in a row. It was only the 2nd time in NHL history that had happened. The first was in 1917–1918.

HOCKEY MEMORIES
Patrick lists his favorite hockey moment as winning a gold medal with Team Canada at the 2010 Vancouver Winter Olympic Games.

2013–2014 STATS

GP	G	A	PTS	PIM
82	33	37	70	18

San Jose Sharks' 1st pick, 2nd overall, in 1997 NHL Entry Draft
1st NHL Team, Season: San Jose Sharks, 1997–1998
Born: September 15, 1979, in Aneroid, Saskatchewan
Position: Left Wing
Shoots: Left
Height: 1.88 m (6'2")
Weight: 100 kg (220 lbs.)

T.J. OSHIE

ST. LOUIS BLUES

Becoming a top-level pro in the National Hockey League is something that takes years. It's not like a player puts on his NHL sweater for the first time and then stops developing. Sometimes a player might have to become physically stronger than he was in college or junior hockey. There are times when a player may have to adjust his game, for example, becoming a two-way player rather than just a goal scorer. Almost every player will tell you that he has to work harder than he ever has.

"I just always kind of played hockey and looked at it being a fun thing," says T.J. "I think maybe I was just getting by on my skill. But, when I got here, I realized that my skill only took me so far. I've become more of a student of the game."

T.J.'s game has never really been just about scoring. Last season was the first time in his pro career that he hit the 20-goal mark. His game is a well-rounded one. He hits harder than most players and has developed into a very good passer and playmaker. Last season was his best ever in the NHL, and he hit career highs with 39 assists and 60 points. His maturity as a player earned him a spot on the U.S. Olympic Team and he accorded himself well playing with and against the best in the world — particularly in the USA's shootout victory against Russia. T.J. was selected to take six of the eight shots; he scored on four of them, including the game-winner!

"Playing in the Olympics is a feeling I can't describe. It means everything to me and my family, and everything I've worked for, for my whole life."

"He's a really talented two-way player," says Blues general manager Doug Armstrong. "There is more to his game than just points. He's a good penalty killer, he brings positive energy to the ice and in the locker room. He's becoming a leader."

And if the last few seasons are any indication, T.J. will continue to work on becoming better still. The better he gets, the better the Blues will be as they push towards the NHL's ultimate prize.

DID YOU KNOW?
Hockey runs in the family for T.J.: cousins Gary Sargent and Henry Boucha both played in the NHL.

HOCKEY MEMORIES
The day T.J. was drafted he was hanging out with his best pal, barely paying attention to the first round as he didn't expect to go that high in the draft. Suddenly, he got a phone call. "I don't think I understood one word. We were both screaming, we were so happy."

2013–2014 STATS

GP	G	A	PTS	PIM
79	21	39	60	42

St. Louis Blues' 1st choice, 24th overall, in 2005 NHL Entry Draft
1st NHL Team, Season: St. Louis Blues, 2008–2009
Born: December 23, 1986, in Everett, Washington
Position: Right Wing
Shoots: Right
Height: 1.8 m (5'11")
Weight: 85.5 kg (189 lbs.)

ALEX OVECHKIN

WASHINGTON CAPITALS

As much as Alex Ovechkin is the face of the Washington Capitals, to millions of Russian hockey fans in 2014, he was also the face of the Russian Olympic Team in Sochi. Hockey is a massive sport in Russia and fans in that country had been waiting for years for the chance to watch the country's greatest players go for an Olympic gold medal on home ice. As we all know by now, the Russians fell to Finland in the quarter-finals, so Olympic gold — or a medal of any color, for that matter — didn't happen. Alex was the first to admit that he, and the team, didn't meet expectations.

> "Nobody ever tells me to pass them the puck or anything. My job is to score goals, and if I don't shoot the puck, I can't score goals."

"First of all, I want to say sorry to the fans," said Alex a few days after the Olympics were over. "Because it's a once in a lifetime opportunity to represent your country in the Olympics, and you don't get the results, you didn't get any medal, the fans, the media and the people who support Russia, family, were upset. But, life goes on."

Sometimes it's easy to forget that behind every hockey superstar is a real person. As Alex was going through his hockey drama, his father underwent a heart operation. This news was kept from Alex until after the Russian team was eliminated from medal contention. His family, including his father, didn't want him to have to worry about his father's health during such a stressful time.

"As soon as I found out that he's in hospital and he's feeling not that good, I just forget the game against Finland and went to the hospital and spent time with him and saw him. It was great to see him feeling better. That was most important thing."

Despite the struggles of the Russian Olympic Team and his father's health scare, Alex got on with the job of being one of the greatest offensive players in the NHL and won the Rocket Richard Trophy as the league's top goal scorer for the fourth time in his career. It was good to see the face of the Washington Capitals with a big smile on it once again.

DID YOU KNOW?

Last season, on December 20, 2013, Alex scored the 400th goal of his NHL career. He hit the mark in 634 games — 1 game less than the "Russian Rocket," Pavel Bure.

HOCKEY MEMORIES

Alex tells a story about being a young boy in a toy store with his parents. He spied a miniature hockey stick, grabbed onto it, and wouldn't let it go. The rest, as they say, is history.

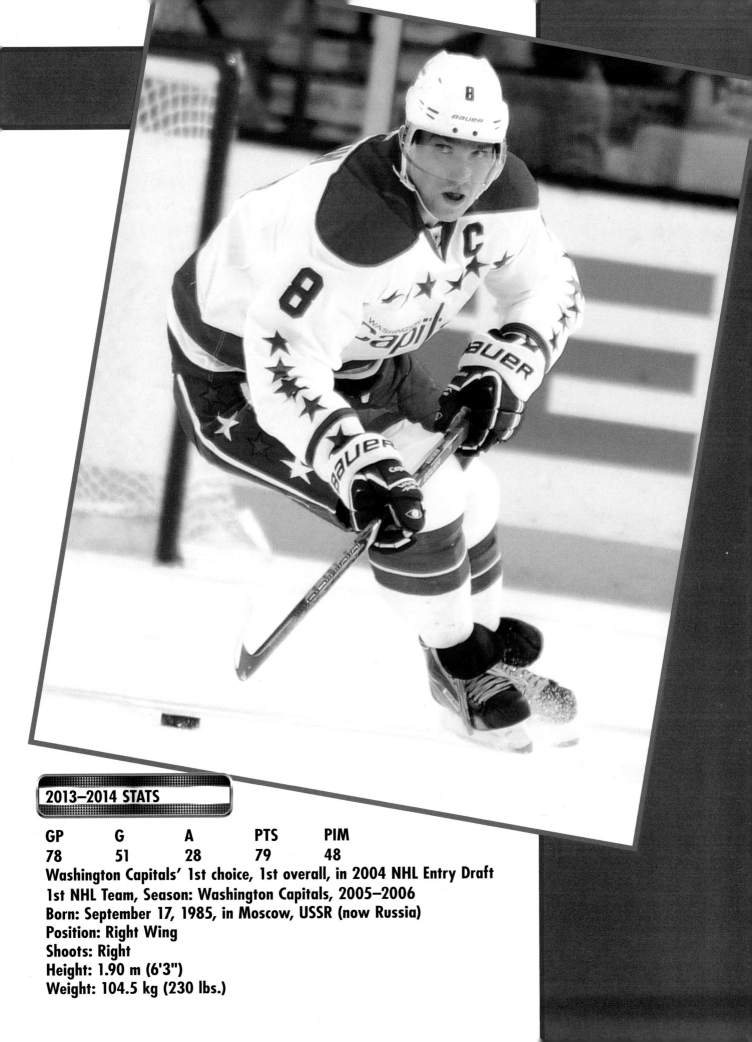

2013–2014 STATS

GP	G	A	PTS	PIM
78	51	28	79	48

Washington Capitals' 1st choice, 1st overall, in 2004 NHL Entry Draft
1st NHL Team, Season: Washington Capitals, 2005–2006
Born: September 17, 1985, in Moscow, USSR (now Russia)
Position: Right Wing
Shoots: Right
Height: 1.90 m (6'3")
Weight: 104.5 kg (230 lbs.)

TUUKKA RASK

BOSTON BRUINS

Pro hockey players are a tough group. Most, when they face a setback, react by taking a positive approach to the situation. After working his way up to being a number one goalie in the top league in Finland, the American Hockey League and, finally, the NHL, Tuukka Rask found himself sitting on the bench in Boston as a back-up goalie. Rask had worked his way to the top job with the Bruins in 2009–2010, finishing with 22 wins and a spectacular 1.97 GAA. But for the next two seasons, the veteran Tim Thomas stepped up and Tuukka found himself struggling at times, and watching more than playing.

"When I think about it now I think that sometimes, to move forward, you have to take a step back," recalls Tuukka. "It [the two seasons as a back-up goalie] was a good learning experience for me to sit on the bench and watch the other guy."

Tuukka's career took a twist after the 2011–2012 season when Thomas decided that he needed a break from the game. That opened the door for Tuukka to re-establish himself as a number one NHL goaltender, and it was an opportunity he took advantage of to the utmost.

"I remember that people doubted me, whether I could carry the load as a number one guy through the year," says Tuukka.

"I'd really rather not talk about myself or my game. Let other people do that if they want. I don't like 'pumping my own tires.'"

Tuukka got the job done, and then some. He was one of the top goalies in the NHL during the shortened 2012–2013 season, including an excellent run to the Stanley Cup Final. Last season Tuukka was even better, winning a career-high 36 games and playing in the Olympic Games for Finland, then backstopping the Bruins through to a second-round, seven-game series loss against Montreal. His great season was capped when he was named the Vezina Trophy winner as the NHL's top goalie.

Have there been a few setbacks along the way for the 27-year-old goalie? Absolutely. But those setbacks have made him better, and right now he's one of the best.

DID YOU KNOW?

Tuukka is one of only two goalies in NHL history to assist on a game-winning overtime goal in the playoffs. The assist came on Miroslav Satan's winner against Buffalo in game four of the 2010 Eastern Conference quarter-final.

HOCKEY MEMORIES

Tuukka has a Stanley Cup ring from 2011, but he earned it as Tim Thomas's back-up. Even though they lost (to Chicago in 6 games), the 2013 Stanley Cup run was much more memorable for Rask. He played in all 22 of the Bruins' post-season games.

2013–2014 STATS

GP	W	L	OT	GAA	SO
58	36	15	6	2.04	7

Toronto Maple Leafs' 1st choice, 21st overall, in 2005 NHL Entry Draft
1st NHL Team, Season: Boston Bruins, 2007–2008
Born: March 10, 1987, in Savonlinna, Finland
Position: Goaltender
Catches: Left
Height: 1.88 m (6'2")
Weight: 84 kg (185 lbs.)

P.K. Subban

MONTREAL CANADIENS

When you watch your favorite NHL player out on the ice living his dream, you should keep in mind that there are parents also living their dream when they watch their son play. Last season, during the annual Montreal Canadiens father-son road trip, P.K. Subban's father, Karl, expressed the feelings of many hockey parents: "I look at it as my son had a dream of playing in the NHL, but people forget that the fathers have dreams too."

"I don't think you ever focus on being rewarded as being the best; I think you just focus on trying to be the best every day at what you can do."

The dream has been on the fast track for P.K. and his family and fans in the last few seasons. As a rookie in 2010–2011, P.K. led all Montreal defensemen in scoring. He did the same in his sophomore season and then, in his third professional season, P.K. was named winner of the James Norris Memorial Trophy as the top defenseman in the NHL. It was the sixth time that a Canadiens defenseman had won the award, but it had been 24 years since one (Hall of Famer Chris Chelios) had been so honored.

"The year he won it [the Norris Trophy] was the year I was born," said P.K., "and to think I'm the sixth defenseman in the history of the Montreal Canadiens to win it, makes it a tremendous honor."

P.K. was also honored last season to be part of Canada's gold medal team at the Olympic Winter Games. Despite being the reigning Norris Trophy winner, he didn't take a regular shift for most of the tournament. But P.K. wasn't bothered at all. He did whatever was asked of him and, in the end, was rewarded along with his teammates for the commitment and hard work.

Perhaps the coolest thing about P.K.'s NHL journey so far is that he's lived that dream with the team he and his father cheered for when he was a boy.

"I grew up a Canadiens fan; my father came to Canada and became a Canadiens fan and I grew up watching the team, which just makes it that much more special."

DID YOU KNOW?

P.K.'s parents come from two very non-hockey countries. His father, Karl, moved to Canada from Jamaica; his mother, Maria, is originally from Montserrat.

HOCKEY MEMORIES

When he was a young boy, P.K. and his dad would spend hours playing in the late-night shinny games that still take place on the big outdoor rink in front of Toronto's City Hall. They'd finish the night with a slice of pizza before heading home for bed.

GP	G	A	PTS	PIM
82	10	43	53	81

Montreal Canadiens' 3rd choice, 43rd overall, in 2007 NHL Entry Draft

1st NHL Team, Season: Montreal Canadiens, 2010–2011

Born: May 13, 1989, in Toronto, Ontario

Position: Defense

Shoots: Right

Height: 1.83 m (6'0")

Weight: 93.5 kg (206 lbs.)

JOHN TAVARES

It was all going so well, and then, suddenly, the excellent season John Tavares was putting together came to a crashing halt. The Islanders' star player suffered a season-ending knee injury while playing for Canada at the Olympic Games. Some said that the injury was a good example of why NHL players should not take part in the Olympics. John didn't share those views.

"For me, as a player, I think it's important for us to play," said John after he returned home. "There's always that concern [getting injured] any time you step on the ice. This [being part of a gold medal effort at the Olympics] goes right up there, if not the top for accomplishments for me."

If there had been any doubt that the Islanders were building their team around the young superstar, they were put to rest when he was named captain prior to the start of last season. John then went out and did what he does best: score points. Prior to the knee injury, John was on pace for his best season in the NHL. He was tops on the Islanders and third in league scoring with 24 goals, 42 assists for 66 points.

"He makes our team go," says Islanders coach Jack Capuano. "I'd put him right up there with some of the top guys in this league. You look at guys like Crosby and Ovechkin; it'd be pretty tough not to put him in that category. He's the face of the Islanders."

> "We have a great group and we're only going to get where we want by working hard and leaning on one another."

Scoring has always been there for John, going back to his junior hockey days when he rattled off three 100-point seasons in a row. But he's had to work on his defensive game and his skating.

"To play professional hockey and to try to be one of the best in the league, you have to be good on both sides of the puck," says John. "My play away from the puck is something that I've really worked hard on."

With a recovered and motivated John Tavares back in the lineup, the Islanders and their fans have lots to look forward to this season.

DID YOU KNOW?
John was deemed to be "an exceptional player" and given special status to be drafted into junior hockey as a 15-year-old. He went on to win the Ontario Hockey League's Rookie of the Year award.

HOCKEY MEMORIES
John can remember being three years old and learning to skate with his dad. He also remembers his mom driving him "everywhere, so I could play."

GP	G	A	PTS	PIM
59	24	42	66	40

New York Islanders' 1st choice, 1st overall, in 2009 NHL Entry Draft
1st NHL Team, Season: New York Islanders, 2009–2010
Born: September 20, 1990, in Mississauga, Ontario
Position: Center
Shoots: Left
Height: 1.85 m (6'1")
Weight: 93 kg (205 lbs.)

CHICAGO BLACKHAWKS

Seven seasons into his NHL career, Jonathan Toews continues to improve and impress. After two shortened seasons, one as a result of concussion symptoms and the other because of the NHL lockout, Toews was back on the mark in 2013–2014, finishing with 68 points — his best offensive season since 2010–2011. He has done all of that, and more, while dealing with the pressure of being the captain of the Chicago Blackhawks.

"Being the captain, having that C on your sweater, there's a lot that goes with that," says Jonathan. "You get a lot of credit when the team's doing well. When the team's not doing so well, you have to be able to accept that responsibility as captain and deal with the questions."

Jonathan was named team captain on February 17, 2008. He was still a couple of months shy of his 20th birthday and was the youngest player ever to be named captain of the Chicago Blackhawks. Some in the hockey world questioned whether that kind of responsibility was too much, too soon. However, others saw an intense and serious player who was mature beyond his years.

"I've always said that I think he becomes more aware every year," says coach Joel Quenneville. "[As an organization] we always said: 'Don't change anything, just play hockey and the rest will take care of itself.'"

"We're just an amazing team to watch, the way we work together. We were just all over them. It's fun to be part of."
— Jonathan talking about Canada's Olympic gold medal win over Sweden

---

To go with the two Stanley Cup Championships, Toews also has two Olympic gold medals with Canada — from 2010 and 2014 — and a World Championship gold medal from 2007. Those three championships — Stanley Cup, Olympic gold and World Championship gold — put him in one of the most elite clubs in hockey: the Triple Gold Club. There are only 24 other players in that group, making it, and Toews, very special indeed.

DID YOU KNOW?
Although he didn't win the Calder Trophy as the NHL's top rookie in 2008 (that honor went to his good friend and teammate Patrick Kane), Toews led all rookies that season with 24 goals.

HOCKEY MEMORIES
One of Jonathan's earliest memories is of Christmas Day when he was two years old. That was the day he received his first pair of skates.

2013–2014 STATS

GP	G	A	PTS	PIM
76	28	40	68	34

Chicago Blackhawks' 1st choice, 3rd overall, in 2006 NHL Entry Draft
1st NHL Team, Season: Chicago Blackhawks, 2007–2008
Born: April 29, 1988, in Winnipeg, Manitoba
Position: Center
Shoots: Left
Height: 1.88 m (6'2")
Weight: 94.5 kg (208 lbs.)

REFEREE SIGNALS

Do you know what is happening when the referee stops play and makes a penalty call? If you don't, then you're missing an important part of the game. The referee can call different penalties that result in anything from playing a man short for two minutes to having a player kicked out of the game.

Here are some of the most common referee signals. Now you'll know what penalties are being called against your team.

Boarding
Checking an opponent into the boards in a violent way.

Charging
Checking an opponent in a violent way as a result of skating or charging at him.

Cross-checking
Striking an opponent with the stick, while both hands are on the stick and both arms are extended.

Elbowing
Checking an opponent with an elbow.

High-sticking
Striking an opponent with the stick, which is held above shoulder height.

Holding
Holding back an opponent with the hands or arms.

Hooking
Using the blade of the stick to hold back an opponent.

Icing
Shooting the puck across the opposing team's goal line from one's own side of the rink. Called only if the opposing player touches the puck first.

Interference
Holding back an opponent who does not have the puck in play.

Kneeing
Using a knee to hold back an opponent.

Misconduct
A ten-minute penalty – the longest type called. Usually for abuse of an official.

Roughing
Shoving or striking an opponent.

REFEREE SIGNALS

Slashing
Using the stick to strike an opponent.

Spearing
Poking an opponent with the blade of the stick.

Slow whistle
The official waits to blow his whistle because of a delayed offside or delayed penalty call. Done while the opposing team has control of the puck.

Tripping
Tripping an opponent with the stick, a hand or a foot.

Unsportsmanlike conduct
Showing poor sportsmanship toward an opponent. For example: biting, pulling hair, etc.

Wash-out
Goal not allowed.

FINAL TEAM STANDINGS 2013–2014

EASTERN CONFERENCE

Atlantic Division

Team	GP	W	L	OT	PTS
BOSTON	82	54	19	9	117
TAMPA BAY	82	46	27	9	101
MONTREAL	82	46	28	8	100
DETROIT	82	39	28	15	93
OTTAWA	82	37	31	14	88
TORONTO	82	38	36	8	84
FLORIDA	82	29	45	8	66
BUFFALO	82	21	51	10	52

Metropolitan Division

Team	GP	W	L	OT	PTS
PITTSBURGH	82	51	24	7	109
NY RANGERS	82	45	31	6	96
PHILADELPHIA	82	42	30	10	94
COLUMBUS	82	43	32	7	93
WASHINGTON	82	38	30	14	90
NEW JERSEY	82	35	29	18	88
CAROLINA	82	36	35	11	83
NY ISLANDERS	82	34	37	11	79

WESTERN CONFERENCE

Pacific Division

Team	GP	W	L	OT	PTS
ANAHEIM	82	54	20	8	116
SAN JOSE	82	51	22	9	111
LOS ANGELES	82	46	28	8	100
PHOENIX	82	37	30	15	89
VANCOUVER	82	36	35	11	83
CALGARY	82	35	40	7	77
EDMONTON	82	29	44	9	67

Central Division

Team	GP	W	L	OT	PTS
COLORADO	82	52	22	8	112
ST. LOUIS	82	52	23	7	111
CHICAGO	82	46	21	15	107
MINNESOTA	82	43	27	12	98
DALLAS	82	40	31	11	91
NASHVILLE	82	38	32	12	88
WINNIPEG	82	37	35	10	84

GP = Games played; W = Wins; L = Losses; OT = Overtime; PTS = Points

Top Ten Points Leaders 2013–2014

PLAYER	TEAM	GP	G	A	P	S	S%
1 SIDNEY CROSBY	PITTSBURGH	80	36	68	104	259	13.9
2 RYAN GETZLAF	ANAHEIM	77	31	56	87	204	15.2
3 CLAUDE GIROUX	PHILADELPHIA	82	28	58	86	223	12.6
4 TYLER SEGUIN	DALLAS	80	37	47	84	294	12.6
5 COREY PERRY	ANAHEIM	81	43	39	82	280	15.4
6 PHIL KESSEL	TORONTO	82	37	43	80	305	12.1
7 TAYLOR HALL	EDMONTON	75	27	53	80	250	10.8
8 ALEX OVECHKIN	WASHINGTON	78	51	28	79	386	13.2
9 JOE PAVELSKI	SAN JOSE	82	41	38	79	225	18.2
10 JAMIE BENN	DALLAS	81	34	45	79	279	12.2

GP = Games played; G = Goals; A = Assists; P = Points;
S = Shots; S% = Percentage

Top Ten Goalies — Total Wins 2013–2014

PLAYER	TEAM	GP	W	L	OT	SA%	GA	GAA
1 SEMYON VARLAMOV	COLORADO	63	41	14	6	.927	146	2.41
2 MARC-ANDRE FLEURY	PITTSBURGH	64	39	18	5	.915	150	2.37
3 ANTTI NIEMI	SAN JOSE	64	39	17	7	.913	149	2.39
4 BEN BISHOP	TAMPA BAY	63	37	14	7	.924	133	2.23
5 TUUKKA RASK	BOSTON	58	36	15	6	.930	115	2.04
6 CAREY PRICE	MONTREAL	59	34	20	5	.927	134	2.32
7 HENRIK LUNDQVIST	NY RANGERS	63	33	24	5	.920	144	2.36
8 KARI LEHTONEN	DALLAS	65	33	20	10	.919	153	2.41
9 STEVE MASON	PHILADELPHIA	61	33	18	7	.917	145	2.50
10 COREY CRAWFORD	CHICAGO	59	32	16	10	.917	128	2.26

GP = Games played; W = Wins; L = Losses; OT = Overtime and/or Shut-Out Losses;
SA% = Save percentage; GA = Goals Against; GAA = Goals-Against Average

END-OF-SEASON STATS

Countdown to the Cup 2014–2015

EASTERN CONFERENCE

STANLEY CUP FINAL

CONFERENCE FINAL

ROUND TWO

ROUND ONE

THE CHAMPION:

WESTERN CONFERENCE

CONFERENCE FINAL

ROUND TWO

ROUND ONE

NHL AWARDS

Here are some of the major NHL awards for individual players. Fill in your selection for each award and then fill in the name of the actual winner of the trophy.

HART MEMORIAL TROPHY
Awarded to the player judged to be the most valuable to his team. Selected by the Professional Hockey Writers Association.

2014 winner: **Sidney Crosby**

Your choice for 2015: _____

The winner: _____

ART ROSS TROPHY
Awarded to the player who leads the league in scoring points at the end of the regular season.

2014 winner: **Sidney Crosby**

Your choice for 2015: _____

The winner: _____

CALDER MEMORIAL TROPHY
Awarded to the player selected as the most proficient in his first year of competition in the NHL. Selected by the Professional Hockey Writers Association.

2014 winner: **Nathan MacKinnon**

Your choice for 2015: _____

The winner: _____

JAMES NORRIS TROPHY
Awarded to the defense player who demonstrates throughout his season the greatest all-round ability. Selected by the Professional Hockey Writers Association.

2014 winner: **Duncan Keith**

Your choice for 2015: _____

The winner: _____

VEZINA TROPHY
Awarded to the goalkeeper judged to be the best. Selected by the NHL general managers.

2014 winner: **Tuukka Rask**

Your choice for 2015: _____

The winner: _____

MAURICE RICHARD TROPHY

Awarded to the player who scores the highest number of regular-season goals.

2014 winner: **Alex Ovechkin**

Your choice for 2015: _____

The winner: _____

FRANK J. SELKE TROPHY

Awarded to the forward who best excels in the defensive aspects of the game. Selected by the Professional Hockey Writers Association.

2014 winner: **Patrice Bergeron**

Your choice for 2015: _____

The winner: _____

WILLIAM M. JENNINGS TROPHY

Awarded to the goalkeeper(s) who played a minimum of 25 games for the team with the fewest goals scored against it.

2014 winner: **Jonathan Quick**

Your choice for 2015: _____

The winner: _____

CONN SMYTHE TROPHY

Awarded to the player most valuable to his team in the Stanley Cup Playoffs. Selected by the Professional Hockey Writers Association.

2014 winner: **Justin Williams**

Your choice for 2015: _____

The winner: _____

LADY BYNG MEMORIAL TROPHY

Awarded to the player judged to have exhibited the best sportsmanship combined with a high standard of playing ability. Selected by the Professional Hockey Writers Association.

2014 winner: **Ryan O'Reilly**

Your choice for 2015: _____

The winner: _____

BILL MASTERTON MEMORIAL TROPHY

Awarded to the player who best exemplifies the qualitites of perseverance, sportsmanship and dedication to hockey. Selected by the Professional Hockey Writers Association.

2014 winner: **Dominic Moore**

Your choice for 2015: _____

The winner: _____

AUTHOR'S ACKNOWLEDGEMENTS: Thanks to NHL.com, NHLPA.com, the Hockey Hall of Fame, and the personal websites of players profiled as well as IIHF.com, hockeydb.com and eliteprospects.com for additional sources of information.

Author photo: Andre Ringuette/HHOF-IIHF Images

Illustrations by Bill Dickson

Photo credits:
Byfuglien: Mark Buckner/NHL via Getty Images Sport
Crosby: Jonathan Kozub/NHL via Getty Images Sport
Filppula: Kirk Irwin/Getty Images Sport
Getzlaf: Derek Leung/Getty Images Sport
Hertl: Lance King/Getty Images Sport
Karlsson: Scott Audette/NHL via Getty Images Sport
Keith: Norm Hall/NHL via Getty Images Sport
Kessel: Graig Abel/NHL via Getty Images Sport
MacKinnon: Paul Bereswill/Getty Images Sport
Marleau: Ronald C. Modra/Sports Imagery via Getty Images Sport
Oshie: Gregg Forwerck/NHL via Getty Images Sport
Ovechkin: Brian Babineau/NHL via Getty Images Sport
Price: Richard Wolowicz/Getty Images Sport
Rask: Paul Bereswill/Getty Images Sport
Subban: Bruce Bennett/Getty Images Sport
Tavares: Joel Auerbach/Getty Images Sport
Toews: Bill Wippert/NHL via Getty Images Sport

www.scholastic.ca

ISBN 978-1-4431-3364-7
Copyright © 2014 by Scholastic Canada Ltd.
All rights reserved.

No part of this publication may be reproduced or stored in a retrieval system, or transmitted in any form or by any means, electronic, mechanical, recording, or otherwise, without written permission of the publisher, Scholastic Canada Ltd., 604 King Street West, Toronto, Ontario M5V 1E1, Canada. In the case of photocopying or other reprographic copying, a licence must be obtained from Access Copyright (Canadian Copyright Licensing Agency), 1 Yonge Street, Suite 800, Toronto, Ontario M5E 1E5 (1-800-893-5777).

6 5 4 3 2   Printed in Canada   118   14 15 16 17

FSC
www.fsc.org
MIX
Paper from responsible sources
FSC® C011825